We are not your metaphor.

a disability poetry anthology

Zoeglossia Fellows
editor

SQUARES & REBELS
Minneapolis, MN

In Gratitude

The publisher is grateful to Connie Voisine, Sheila Black, and Jennifer Bartlett for enabling the first Zoeglossia conference to happen, and to the inaugural Zoeglossia Fellows for sharing their work in support of this fundraising venture. (Profits from the sale of this book will be donated to Zoeglossia.) The publisher also appreciates the support of this project—in ways large and small—provided by Eric Thomas Norris, Scott Holl, and David Cummer.

Acknowledgments

The following reprints have appeared elsewhere:

Elizabeth Theriot: "Sestina for Greeting My Body," *Ghost Proposal.*

Naomi Ortiz: "Open Mic Nite," *VIDA Review.*

Genevieve Arlie: "Acute Effects of Chronic Heroism," *Nat. Brut.*; "Of late, all creatures," Finalist, The 47th Annual Scott College Writers Festival; "Ferryman's Matin," *Columbia Journal Online*; and "From the Tree," *Flyway: Journal of Writing and Environment.*

Copyright

The Fellows

Kathi Wolfe

Metaphorically Speaking

Excerpted from the first Zoeglossia keynote speech

Like many poets and writers with disabilities, I've run into ableism—overt and subtle disability-based prejudice. Barriers of access and attitudes.

There was the time I was in a poetry workshop at a university in Washington, D.C. Before the first class began, the teacher spoke to me. "You can stay in the class," he told me, "as long as your blindness doesn't make unreasonable demands or upset the other students." I was furious, but I stayed in the class.

Sometimes ableism is so embedded in our culture that it's hard to recognize that it's there. Getting people to be aware of it is like asking them to think about the air that we breathe in. It's subtle; it's often unconscious and not meant to be hurtful. Yet it often perpetuates untrue and demeaning images and stereotypes. That can fester and, without conscious awareness, form misperceptions about disabled people.

For poets, one example of this is the ableist metaphors used so often in poetry to describe disabilities or those of us with disabilities. How often have you read poems that use blindness as a metaphor for spiritual ignorance, unthinking faith, or moral failings? Or deafness used as a metaphor for isolation, aloneness—a failure to emotionally communicate? Think: world of darkness. Deaf ears. Crippling rage.

I don't want to come down too hard or to rigidly on this. Our language wouldn't be language without metaphors. I doubt that we could write poems without metaphors. Different poets have different takes on this. Some poets don't mind the metaphors. I sometimes try to reclaim the metaphors—to use metaphors in a way that's authentic to my disability. But it's fair, I think, to say that too often all of us, including me, tend to use such metaphors without thinking.

Accessibility: I don't know any disabled poet who hasn't had to deal at some point with some type of inaccessibility. From a lack of a ramp leading up to a stage to a lack of sign language interpreters. For me, as someone with low vision, inaccessibility takes the form of inaccessible web sites and submission portals. What has this meant in practical terms? I have to have someone submit my work for me. This often takes extra time—because people can only assist me when their schedule permits. Fortunately my friends are kind and way helpful! But I sometimes miss submission deadlines.

Kathi Wolfe

I share these moments from my life with you not because they're extraordinary, but because I believe that many poets with disabilities have had similar experiences.

Like so many of us, I'm not only a poet with a disability. I belong to more than one community. Lambda Literary Foundation is an LGBTQ group that fosters queer writers. In 2008, I was a Lambda Literary Foundation Emerging Writer fellow and attended a Lambda Lit retreat for the fellows. I found the experience to be energizing and helpful: I got to be part of some workshops let by queer poets. It made me feel that I wasn't alone: I was part of a tribe.

Over the years, I've been so lucky! I've worked with, read the work of, and formed friendships with wonderful poets with disabilities, from Raymond Luczak to Jennifer Bartlett to Ellen McGrath Smith. This has enriched my life personally and creatively. I am honored to have my work included in such groundbreaking anthologies as *QDA: A Queer Disability Anthology* edited by Raymond Luczak (Squares & Rebels) and *Beauty Is a Verb: The New Poetry of Disability* edited by Michael Northern, Sheila Black, and Jennifer Bartlett (Cinco Puntos Press). These anthologies have not only brought the work of poets with disabilities into the wider culture; they've also fostered a sense of community.

Yet, despite this progress, I've still felt, as I think many of us have felt, isolated in the poetry world—that we poets with disabilities haven't had a seat at the poetry table. One night years ago, as I sat with Sheila Black while munching chips and sipping my margarita, my feelings became focused into a longing, a dream: Could we create a group for poets with disabilities that would be similar to Lambda Literary Foundation or Cave Canem? A group that would help us to find our tribe. That would help us to be a force—to be seen and heard in the poetry world. We could speak as a group about accessibility. It's more difficult for editors, the academy, and folks coordinating poetry readings and events—to ignore a group than to turn away from an individual. That would give us a chance to discuss the many questions of disability identity, reflect on disability history, and muse about our craft.

After visiting with Sheila, I put my dream aside and got sucked up into the nitty-gritty of my life. But Sheila didn't forget about my dream. A shout-out to Sheila Black, Jennifer Bartlett, and Connie Voisine for making Zoeglossia happen.

I don't think there's never been anything like this for poets with disabilities. Let's make history! Let's make art.

WE ARE NOT YOUR METAPHOR

The Fellows

Innate

My hips, like the multiverse, are in ceaseless amplification. Each elegant face of love my hips have carried spread me out a bit more. Bare bones remember my unborn whether it rains or is cold. My children are uniquely human yet alien to me. Quixotic stares between us may last through infinity. The expanse of (space) time is not on our side ... and I had approached the event horizon. I tasted blood in the air around me. Those I miscarried in my youth still hold a place for me in dreams. We are more real than atomic mass. Everything alive seems so finite after birth.

Viktoria Valenzuela

Cosmic

I breathe deep
Flaring nostrils
Clouds of sacred smoke   open like
new eyes.

We're hungry
Awoken by the stir of a baby, I say
hold me this way in bed.
Hold tight our slippery   softness.

Humanity emerges
from anew.
I see you   happy
my love.

Cosmic bodies spark a life
Clouds open
Pushing forth to sprout like
Agave flowers at the end   of a century

The Poems Before Them

Carried all my babies like poems.
Carried the first one across the ocean
        the next across America.
Two more were cut out of me, right here, in Texas.

I am like the mother shark washed up on a beach
Across the ocean,
        or maybe, this side of America,
and the tourists of paradise have cut me open.

They take out the babies.
One by one
        baby sharks swim away from their mother,
            the shore,
                the tourists of paradise.

They go on to live their lives beyond a mother-bled ocean
        —like countless poems before them.
Not even the wind comes from the same direction anymore.
        Every speech is done with a dying breath.
            Mother creatures like us have sunburnt bodies.

Across the country, Inuit elders read the stars.
        They've written letters to NASA that tell of our shifted sky
            Just as words in language have changed over our lifetime,
                The Sky has changed.

From a room in a room   I inhale.
        saying, goodbye.
From my bed   I exhale,
        saying, thank you.
From my womb   —unfolding
        The sky has shifted ...

            She has left her post.

Viktoria Valenzuela

I carried all my babies like shark's dreams.
Carried the first one across the ocean
      the next across America,
Two more carved out of me, right here, in Texas.

I am a shark washed up on the beach.
Or maybe, a mother-poet is sleeping beside her newborn.
Across the ocean a mother shark swam,
From Coatlicue to Chaxiraxi,
mother to mother,
Where the tourists of paradise have cut her open.

An oean of mother's blood shed.
One by one, babies drift away
From a double pink slit in the womb,
The shore, the tourists,   my half woke dreams.

Swell Times

In bed, I let it be
Even if I do not make breakfast tacos
Whole wheat tortillas are a no-no.
The ghost of our grandmothers heaving with laughter
Remind that joy is ours to carry on.
The C-section stitches tighten.
I've already passed the floor with him
Kissed him, given milk,
Held him to my chest, patted his tiny diaper.
He spins in his quilt as if still in the womb;
Slow solid steps mean, I smell blood.
The salt of me.
I was built to feed a nation.

This C-section scar
itches like a motherfucker
A two-faced snake lurking between my pubis and the fat of me.
The children
were born fully armed for battle
Pulled against their will to stay snake coiled inside me.
The baby
Drinks the milk I bleed
We lie still in the dark until
The daylight
Warms our sinuous curves
Masa swelling in a bowl under a cover.

Viktoria Valenzuela

We Don't Care About Anything

I run my fingers over the mirror.

In the dust,
       I trace the shape of your aging face
           —over here is your motley of hair ...

Eyes.   Lips.

The room your hard working man is snoring in.
       —his copper penny lips seem to be straining purple, but
His eyebrows are calm
       reminding you of all the love in the world.

This silky is the repose for the living-
                room recliner.

The children we've made,
       asleep in another room, and I am sitting here
            erecting a tableau of our life at midnight ...

                    The movie *Kill Bill* is playing
                      on Television.

I empathize with Uma; as if a she were an undocumented mother
       breaking free of her shallow grave.
           take in all that air, warrior woman!

I've remove our bra,
            scratching the ridge along
once milk heavy breasts,
       six times pregnant belly—
           our back and shoulders also get the scratch.

Rubbing skin, hot and smooth,
       we are alive in that cold mirror.

           We hold countenance under glass.

Dìa de los Muertos

"Leave me / Lying here / cuz' I don't want to go ..." (Veruca Salt)

Later, after you get home from work
After the someone wins the world series
After we are lying in bed giving cariños
And after you admit
You still fear the future me dying
And I admit that I still fear the future you dying
Middle age is not for faint hearts

It's after midnight
On El Dìa de los Muertos,
San Antonio, TX
I've built the altár
For our antepasados
No pan dulce, but hay dulce
y rosas

In bed,
Even in our sleep, we hold hands
Giving thanks is done
I kiss your arm
Our palms rub together
And our legs extend (braiding) as if root systems of trees
still in conversation

After we die,
We've promised the other, we'll be buried together
Just like this ... coiled in a sac of Chimayo dirt
Under the sapling of a pecan tree.

Viktoria Valenzuela

Dear Stars,

I met you in bed, unaware that I was one of you. The dust of my dust is your dust too. I am at once inside infinity while you are at the middle of me ... and all around me.

I can almost taste sparkling champagne (or is it moonlit rain) that celebrates you, child, who was once inside me. Edged with the lathers of memory (though my waters never split without help), I held us in until (... until ... until) birth.

It was a slice (or maybe an explosion) in the body that echoed infinity. The birth of my birth is your birth—really, our birth. In bed, I now sense the holding pattern (of our last baktun) and the doctor has cut at the base of my abdomen. She has pulled our warrior god from me; our crowning jewel. She has sewn me back together with barbed wire. Alone, we three huddle together behind a scrim of certainty.

My body a bridge; our thoughts are thoughts of birth. I close my eyes when the sacred pain of nursing newborn begins. My breasts drip warm milk over the stabbing contractions of womb. I breathe as if in natural labor. All the pain comes after a c-section. Outstretched beside us, an all knowing placenta, the tree of life.

Endlessly, with love,
Momma

I.

Tell them I'm happy and that I struggle with headaches.

Eat pizza for me.   Bring an umbrella.

scapegoat finally is the kind of goat you were

And behind you the window

open   open

Gaia Celeste Thomas

II.

The butter dog licking itself into oblivion.

That swelling in your head, has it going down?

The unhealthiest men came and told me to heal.

I sat at the traffic lights for 10 minutes not knowing I had to come up
to the line.

III.

Overhead helicopters try to save someone.

My feet are burning inside the cotton inside my boots.

I'm mixing cocktails trying to make the afterparty before.

Rattle and clatter where cherries once hung.

Gaia Celeste Thomas

IV.

a pregnant ghost alters the line of the wall

muffins and the impossibility of sleeping with another human being

am I stumbling through basements

are you spider   dreams

1

Cupfuls of bleach restore transparency to the river, while taking the life out of it.

▼

Snow and sugar and blue dye and milk in a hospital pitcher. She can heat water for tea in the microwave.

▼

"The world is an apple made of shit," she says. "And all souls are worms trying to fit through that hole. One at a time."

▼

She makes her bed with a board between one metal cabinet and the other. And there she perches like a bird inspecting the territory of possibility contained within her room. Purple when she escaped and left the bathtub empty of a self. This sort of mental illness of conjecture. They will convict you for composing poems out loud.

2

Disability is a soft border of green around my bedroom. It was a quick job, the piecing him back together — surgery still showed the seams.

▼

White clover cannot be easily shuffled. But still the men come in, make marks in orange, erase them. Anti-myth, anti-homogenization, anti-cell replication. Anti-charity, anti-religion, pro-blood, pro-pack, pro-voice. Pro-damage. Pro-ash.

▼

An organism made of charges between skins: one jumping electric cloud.

▼

To which we never made. Searching for topology the shape of a hollow doughnut. Mustard yellow boots swing toward the gray slide and back by themselves, by themselves. In that bed she is a boy freezing to death on the edge of a cliff.

3

Sugar ants spilling out the bottom of an unlit candle.

▼

Nest of train whistle, birdsong, palm fronds. Batting of egg crate fastened for minimal damage to a host of neural butter lamps braced for impact. And in this aluminum velocity asphalt : anywhere, anywhere.

▼

So then the flesh like a rotisserie skewer: her twisting — underwater. How close to the bone do you carve? What is the rate of attrition as we leave the center, by which our bodies become yours and not ours? What fraction here in the suburbs still belongs? Have I all of my dust? *Ne touche pas.*

▼

Goats ordained me with shit and piss. As we dance any signal sending lighthouse could be your beacon.

Gaia Celeste Thomas

Notes:

Drop the hide of social convention as you enter through the open door frame.

One end to the girl chained to the bed, one end to the typewriter. Cigarette in white petals. Clipboard, check marks, the endless recycling fountain.

As if a jaw were an arm.

Mist of dew in grass at dawn. All through the night watching her small pulse of white thunder flicker at us across the water in jail.

A slug taught me to hear how time and space are legs being torn apart at the crotch.

Fold and twist, create edges where there are none. Slink around the pinkie and then tip outside.

He moves on from acne scabs to sutures, worrying these thin places — and what seeps there slick as gasoline between his fingers.

Her hand [which last braced the handle of a gun] tips the candle right side up.

Insulation, fiber of leg meat, snow.

She told me they were tipping the cup of their bodies up to a mouth in the black wall of oblivion.

All day we are hunting text in a library of scratch marks you can't see.

A lens between her hands, she magnifies the sun into glass.

Dépêche toi. Dépêche toi. Dépêche toi. Dépêche toi.

Haruspex

sometimes I'm shocked like amazed by what comes out my body
taking something of my body with it
murky ecosystem

my body could hold anything
stardust, milk
except it doesn't
I know because I've seen my skin turn over,
its torn ledger

if only I could read a fortune
in the meat and blood

if only fate were static
and my body too

Elizabeth Theriot

Glass

The girl lives in a glass house. Every tread must involve the utmost caution.

Every step an almost-shatter. She tosses and turns at night gingerly on her

crystal bed. She has excellent posture. If she sits she perches. Outside her

walls the world billows and settles like a snapped sheet. She sundials her

body through different rooms to chase warm slices of morning, afternoon,

evening. Her house gulps up the moon and cools before sleep. The quiet is so

quiet it makes her beams brittle. She imagines hardening into a flower vase

and traces her finger along cracks and fractures. She lays on the floor and

imagines looking up at her flattened body. Her body is the softest possible

thing, of this she is certain. She has never lacked a point of comparison. She

has never lacked a comportment of eggshells and soufflé.

Sestina for Greeting My Body

I unfold   my snap-lock altar   saying this is my body
this my body & I   will drink this time
these   the consequences of the spell I cast
in jars of apple   butter crashed, pull up   the root
of the problem   the branches   lengthened inside my jar
& every extra sock, hello. Hello socks   & yes, the burn

yes, hello! Peeping from inside   stocking-holes, I burn
I really do. Really   pulled over, this the ticket   my body
gives me   with a low head-   shake, this jar
ringing 'round my rosy   digestive track.   Hurry it's time
to text back your mother,   hello. Time   to get to the root
of your problems, the nugget of gold   you can't swallow. Lots cast:

40 pieces of silver,   what a deal! Steal   me piles of cast-
off candy, gum printed   with your molars. Money to burn,
cash   to change. Hello, I wasn't   sure which route to root
to remember   where parents live. I do   dig how your body
ferments so well. You don't believe   you'll last a long time
but there it is, your usual plaid   & there my honey in its jar

I pour out, ooh   sticky all over the stove, broken jar-
ring to low-medium,   propose an afternoon to cast
in bronze & burgundy   broke leg & sweeten my tea   high time
to climb inside your mouth,   lite a cigarette & burn
dark on the porch,   almost ready   climb inside my body
under eyes all   palimpsest hello   did you root

for me? Or...?   Hello at 9:00,   Lincoln logs & Jenga,   salty root
haunted knocks   like knees & door not door when it's a jar,
door   a gift   delicious nightmare,   a door-able this body
taking the window,   my window open   & shadows cast
out with the lint & bacteria. Wax is poetic, you burn
pine-scented candles   & never rhyme   & next time

Elizabeth Theriot

you will say *look these were in my pocket the entire time,*
these pieces of your fingers, here, take them before they take root
and grow a phalange-tree in my living room, so maybe burn
them in the bathroom sink with sage, empty out a jar
of frog appendages & eye-of-newt into your seasoned cast-
iron, you know what to do　　　　　& I will serve up my body

this time toward　　　the cauldron, drip drip　　　into the jar
all greasy greasy　　　fat catch a line　　　on the cypress root
hello hello cypress,　　　burn my bark & I'll learn　　　to be a body.

Take Me to Your Leader

I want to need my body less yes am ready
for the alien overlords with their cybernetic parts
who lower me into a tank of strange luminescent fluid
connect wires and press buttons and upload my brain
while all my nonrenewable perishables are replaced
with indestructible metals, sturdy yet pliant synthetic skin,
nerves, other intestinal bits, maybe I'll still even shit
like one of those Baby Born dolls, or maybe I'll be like
a vampire whose particular mythos allows her
to still eat for fun because yes I want all the good parts
of being in a body, the tastes and smells and pleasures
of other life forces inside me, masticated, caressed
the best of both worlds, to live and never die
I will tell the aliens *look! I can write poems!*
I am writing this for you! Please value me, please
save what I never could.

Elizabeth Theriot

An Emergency
with a line from Jessica Suzanne Stokes

I Love becomes Olive becomes Pimento.
Where is the heavy cream, the torn bag of groceries,
the lingering over something new and succulent?
Senior year I drank nothing but almond butter smoothies
each morning. I'm not saying it's like this,
but it's almost like this. Us dog eared and jangling
coffee rings, the cabinet overflowing with tea.

I Love becomes I Louvre becomes a collection of frames.
I've had a certain urge around expensive, precious things
to swing a bat and see how the shattering feels
outside my skin—to break something first, anticipate
the breaking—to snip the sutures before the scar
goes red and leaks unrepentant pus.

#SelfieSaturday

how much of me am i made of pixel really
gingham, moon, juno, lark
magicianess mirror hall
this lipstick
this unbrushed bun
tuck wings
tuck wings
camera 360 and rosy
quick slid illusion meanwhile
three daily steps and
gingham, moon, juno, lark
indentured recipe clicking incantation
what makes me what i
will never have
tuck wings
gingham, moon, juno, lark
i am the processed fibers
raw at every entrance
boiled pour-over
coffee without
crema, rise, willow, ink
hairshirt price on amazon
bamboo nails
made for crucifixion
tuck wings
A/C off and blood
if my stomach was unhuman
shade of teal, violet, I'd feel better
a loud talking spaceship
sleekly dive thru air like
muscle tense, salmon
sweet potato, brussel sprout
crema, rise, willow, ink
tuck wings
and every moving part,
glory me if made
of nothing not necessary

Elizabeth Theriot

After Aubrey and I Text about Our Dying Planet

I lay out old shirts to make cleaning rags
from the flattened shape of my torso,
move the scissors V to hem.

From autopsy descriptions, I recall
this is the most efficient way of opening,
much cleaner than what my fingers tore.

/

I wore some icy blue velvet boots
with a tall chunky heel, thinking
maybe this time, but walking
was like my bones at the edge of collapse,
I tried to picture all the parts holding
me together and couldn't, my feet hurt,
it hurt to walk, it felt like another prophecy.

/

Maybe there is future for me,
all the cement covered in soft layers of moss.

Excerpts from <u>After Versed</u>

Cataclysm like
Catalyst

I remember
To persons no longer
Present

I can say
"Oh, no thank you"
To any of it

I am writing this
Always
And I

Zoe Stoller

A string of notes—
Which inversion?

I imagine myself
Passing
Into phase

I'm looking for a
How-to-write

Zoe Stoller

Obedient
Submissive
In the sun

It was years
So she broke herself
To bits,

But the sense
Of having come full circle
Could not be eliminated
Except where to now

The mind wanders
Far of course

The whole plain
With making fun of meat

Zoe Stoller

Forming a consensus
Leaves out subjectivity

In a rosy glow
With fingers

Instead the frame served
The bath and
The lie

Zoe Stoller

Operation Phantom
In the London pool

The full force
Of the will to live
Is fixed
In fear
Like I used to say

Jessica Suzanne Stokes

New Shoes
after Amy Lowell's "Red Slippers"

Dad drove the impala nervous to the mall.
Only plastic bags were left to leaf the trees.
Greybrown leftovers of snow coated the lot:
where Burlington sold coats to keep each winter
from the body and cars passed on black rubber
tracks to the ground and J.C. Penney propped red
heels in a window display, taking eyes off
people's feet. They were dreaming of stalactites
lovers, direction, rockets, and purchased polish.
I was looking down, imagining shoving
my left foot on a silver Brannock, sliding
to find its size—slide—And Dad is mad he says
about how slowly I lace the thick tan shoes.
"Walk heel—toe, not thud—thud." And I am crying
about how the round brown shoes push on my toes.
And I don't understand how blunt the shoes are,
even as metaphors. And I don't fit in my father's.

Jessica Suzanne Stokes

Dress Normal
after the text of a GAP advertisement on Boston University T-stop, fall 2014

The last time I went to the surgeon he wanted my toe.
I said no.
Before that, he asked if he could put me into a cage,
just my leg,
each bar of the cage would be pushed entirely through my calf
so it could
be periodically tightened. He called it a halo
and said don't
be frightened, we guarantee you'll be normal looking soon.

It's Still Life

there is a mason jar
        rather than   fruit   bowls   or wine
filled with what looks like orange juice
sitting on a booklined desk as the sun shines
down in the small space between the neighboring
apartment building and the end of the window's viewfinder
        I call it sun but it's the greywhite light of winter
                the sun is somewhere
                pinned into the firmament
                behind it
                      they tell us
                          we must trust
the secret to the orange juice is the vodka
or the girl who put the vodka in the orange juice
now just still enough
as she wrestles with her comforter
to count as part of the picture I'm allowed to describe
there is no clock in the room or I could tell you the time
but time is told by opening computers or holding buttons
down long enough to wake up phones
she doesn't wish to know time anyway as the jim beam
she drank keeps her stomach company for awhile
she doesn't wish to wake
up phones or self   even if the dreams go bad
they are some kind of escape
as long as the dreams are distinguishable from this
as long as the dreams kindly remind her of their relationship
yet   inherent distance   from   everything
she can separate them   off   pretend to suspend
disbelief   to comfort them in return for highlighting
their space   through paled comparison

she grabbed the orange juice and the vodka at the party
to make it look like she was there to drink with everyone
not just jim
she isn't a sad drunk   instead

drinking like she dreams
        to see it from another perspective
        to leave it and come back
            traveling without tangible distance
                without maps or at least google directions
                to articulate actual space
            no mileage number to cling to
                or mile markers to count
                    but still further away

you have to be careful about things like liking to drink by yourself
        if only for the viewer's sake
because they might try to stop you
        if you differ too much from the picture of regular
            they've been collaging in their mind
she's fine around friends whose parents
tipped back many too many bottles
or who saw as much violence as she
somewhere other than a screen
they can differentiate
        the softness of her stomach
           from
        the harshness of their truth
they can know sometimes there are days when you escape
sometimes those days can't be facilitated by a CD and a gas pedal
because gas costs too much and walks are too clunky
with broken headphones or icy streets

I've forgotten about the picture
I'm not very good at keeping life still
It's probably because of how close I am to the girl
        asleep on the bed with her fluffy red curls
        shaping into spikes with the help of a pillow
I have the almost same now spikey puffy head
two hours later   about 45 degrees different   no more
I lean a little
sitting clicking on the bed with the computer screen
open to reveal time

she couldn't sleep forever

                              WE ARE NOT YOUR METAPHOR

making this whole thing difficult to write
like drawing someone
who flails too much when they talk
or drawing yourself in a mirror and
trying not to draw yourself drawing
but rather doing something better and
she and I and we probably shouldn't have told you about all this
      if we really want distance
      she can't be me
      writing can't be truth
      and if it is
      it needs to be someone else's truth
      which is good to know but not particularly relevant

when they take a Stephen King novel and eliminate
the supernatural for the screen
as if it needs to be more real
than it already was
they've forgotten we all need to travel
they've forgotten they are we   or
maybe they don't watch what they make

I'm looking out the space
between the building and the molding of the window
where the lit grey sky is light enough to write by
hoping one time when the firmament spins the sun away
and the other side of the window is dark enough
to leave my reflected face to be seen by me
I won't feel compelled to write to further
her away   from me

Jessica Suzanne Stokes

Student Art Showcase at Our Lady of the Lake

The World Without Balance costs
50 dollars.
The World Without Balance sits
atop a white wooden stand and
has a copper painted plastic base on top of that.
Surely there's a metaphor here as roots become lightning bolts.
Fractals take over underworlds and multiply into multiplied
meanings ...
But the World Without Balance isn't as heavy as all that.
Light and easy to spin
away again.
The materials cost as much as a globe costs
when it still has the Soviet Union on it and
it is tucked into the corner of a thrift store
waiting for someone to switch out its 10 dollar label
with the 2 dollar label on a nearby deck of cards.
Shuffle and spin and shuffle and spin and ...
pick it up kids. That's the game isn't it?

WE ARE NOT YOUR METAPHOR

Fala*

I am a dog of blackout
curtains, who sniffs at
the somber hive of sharp
creased pant legs. I
belong with the man on wheels, who
rubs my neck exactly right.
At sea, sailors snip my coat.
We live in rooms of the blocked
out sun. When he slides from
the chair, long useless bones,
I am the only creature present,
smelling his ear, offering my damp
callow nose.

---

* the most photographed dog of the 1940s

Margaret Ricketts

Spastic Poetry

The line
is broken
staggers
muscle spasm
not a metaphor
scream for help
ragged wave
breaking
on shore.

My Mother

I was never able
to suckle at her
breast, yet she
willed it into me
night and day-
live, exist, be
well. Fifty years
later, that current
passes between
the two of us,
still.

Margaret Ricketts

Hegemony

is the belief that
any human force
can alter
the shifting
plates
of the earth.
This is a
poetically
fit
scream
for help

The Addict

a dry leaf
clings to
a winter
stripped
branch.
a dead man
is trying
to dig out
the roots
with a rusted
trowel.

Margaret Ricketts

The Coffee Speaks to Him Now

The coffee, Seattle's Best, the
substance we bicker over each
morning, the coffee speaks to
him now. The coffee cup with
mallards is talking to him now.
I hope the voice isn't cruel, isn't
speaking of the web of dangers
surrounding his frail body. But he
still knows, the fear of falling leaves last,
can he feel my fierce tenderness?

Porter Street Cafe

Every eighteen months or so, we
have one of these foolish, fragrant
lunches, thick potato soup for me,
salmon and a glass of Chardonnay
for you, back in remission again. I
drink my diet Coke, not recalling when
I drank nothing else, when vertigo
cockscrewed and twisted in my
brain, when I needed a friend to help
from the bed to the bathtub. Colleen,
Eric, Diane. Driving me to the neurologist, the CT scan. So much
shitwork when someone seriously
loses it. I've been well for months now.

You went to Kroger's yesterday and put
away the food yourself. Two months
I sat in a spare wheelchair and watched
you lie on your side, too desolate for talk or touch or water. You are back
and vivid again. We resolve never to
get overextended again, not to get mad
at ourselves when we always do.

Look—a chilly April morning and the Bradford pear just in bloom.

Margaret Ricketts

The Mansion

zoeglossia is many things—a poem
exploding across the face and fingers
of ASL, intellect inscribed silently
in the air, the chairs and floors of the
mansion we built with our own hands.

A Journey Beyond the Edge

There is always an edge
a place where dark meets light
a place where wind and spirit rendezvous mountainside
a place where meshing ridgelines carve the bone structure
of the Earth's ever twisting spine

There is always an edge
where storm clouds gather
and sun still shines
a buildup of opposites,
clashing, to unleash thunderous sound
only offering brief moments of illumination

There is always an edge between future and past
   This moment right here
With sunlight streaming, no wind blowing
and silence, so rare for the middle of the city

There is always an edge
where the recognition of self, faces confusion
where inner fire greets the soothing well of wisdom
  Even if I'm left with steam cascading upwards, obscuring my truth

I am constantly asking myself
  where is my edge
Between my yard and the neighbors'
Between fear and faith
Before one decision spirals into another
Between what I can and cannot control

The desert offers little guidance
everything living intertwined above ground or below

But then a passing cloud releases a drop of water,
  clearly outlined on dry desert dirt
Borders widen where dark wet brown meets dry tan sand
Where roots grown in faith, welcome moisture, drawing it in

Naomi Ortiz

Or where beetle antennas delicately gather
what liquid remains,
to carry, balanced with gravity and surface tension

    This drop of water
        Whose edges touch the entire world

Outdoor Elevator Going Down

I pause, enjoying the
dark clouds hung low
over the mountains.
The gusting wind tunneling
between the office buildings.

Lifting all my hair,
force slams into body.
Face forward, I feel
like I am charging
into the storm.

I stay here playing
with the wind, until
this older man creeps up,
and startled, I push
the elevator button for "down."

Going into the elevator,
the man starts to complain
about the rain.

Before the doors slide closed,
he points to his fancy, yellow,
expensive car, and exclaims,
"I just washed it of course!"

With a laugh, I thank him,
for that *just washed* car luring the rain.

But he continues, complaining
his wife swore he was safe!
Then looks me straight in the face,
and says, "Women don't know anything."

I had just been sparring with wind,
birthing a rare spring desert storm.

Naomi Ortiz

This man, doesn't intimidate me.

Locking my eyes, with his.
I say firmly, "We know lots of things."

My gaze lingers,
he looks everywhere inside this metal box,
but at me.
I revel in this awkward silence,
as we drop slowly to the street.

The elevator shudders in a pop of rise,
my conspirator, settling itself ever so slowly,
taking pause, before dinging, "ground floor."

All the while the man squirms
to escape the fury of this storm,
which caught him by surprise.

Naomi Ortiz

Addressing the Plumbing

Underneath the sink, carved into the wall
is a secret passageway.
Built long ago
to move that which is
ready to be washed away.

Unattended, movement slows.
Clogged by all I discard
Tiny pieces of me, cling to
one another

But life is a process of taking in
and letting go, letting flow.
       Sometimes, I must punch through
and clear out
that which is stuck.

Chain uncoiled,
runs the length of my everyday habits,
drawing out all which stops me
from releasing, from moving on.

A necessary, but costly consequence,
of day-to-day living, in this house of mine.

Naomi Ortiz

Ablesplaining   Part 2,749

"Yes, we are a festival about celebrating and embracing the diversity in our community. No, we don't have a ramp for the stage ... I don't see a problem with having the founder of the festival MC from the ground. Besides, he's the only person in a wheelchair that's part of the festival."
When diversity is celebrated—except for disability.

A festival about celebrating culture,
that uses long plastic boxes pitched over winding electrical
    cords.
Speed-bumps everywhere.

I normally ram them at high speeds using momentum to slide
    over,
but in the crowds, I must go slow,
and I get stuck.
The box is higher than the clearance of my scooter.
I am stranded teetering on top, my wheels no longer
    touch the ground.

Abruptly, I am being shoved in the back—pushed out of my
    chair by some unknown person
        I can't see.
        I am being tipped to the side by a
        second man yanking on the scooter—I am falling—
            and I scream,

"STOP!"
No one listens.

"STOP TOUCHING ME!" I yell into the crowd of passing
    people.
No one listens.

Angrily, the man yanking on my scooter shouts, "WHAT! I
    was only trying to help!"
His first time talking to me is a dismissal ablesplaining
    away my anger.

WE ARE NOT YOUR METAPHOR

But this gets into all the ways I am touched without consent.
My body taken over by a stranger.
**Where even when I'm yelling, surrounded by a crowd of
    people,**
no one registers there's a problem.

Naomi Ortiz

Open Mic Nite

At the poetry slam,
I am alone in a crowd,
stuffed to one side.
Drunk 20-somethings use my shoulder like a handrail to climb over my
    legs, intent on moving forward.
I am craning my body to see around the butts of the standing forms,
hoping to catch a glimpse of light, of movement, an expression to go with
    the words.

At least, this time, I got in the door.

In my wheelchair—
At best, I'm seen as someone to absorb, to witness.
At worst, I take up a lot of space, I distract.

Neither are how I see myself.

Tucked in my bag are poems, words formed out of dry desert air.
But ... that dense feeling, I have in my chest,
the one which tries to create solid strength out of sadness,
lets me know there's no way through.

No way through
the crowd,
the chairs,
the steps,
the courtyard dirt
the rocks
No way to
the sign-up sheet
or for that matter,
no way to
roll onto stage.

No chance to pitch my words into the room,
for them to ride alongside the others,
permeating people's bodies,   out into the night.

Intaglio

The ink of that gruff morning air from the shore of Lake Superior filled the grooves of my soul trapped in a printing plate not of my own making. I saw the atlas of my life cut down to its most unflattering dimensions and compressed by the weight of a roller made heavy by fear and my ridiculous ache to be loved. I had slept the night before in a sleeping bag with my other cabin mates but they had already disappeared, leaving behind wisps of fog where they'd slept. Why hadn't they woken me? Hadn't they known the depth of my orphanhood? Faceless ghosts bigger than pine trees hovered in infinitesimal layers of white and gray. I felt their eyes inquiring as to my loneliness, but I was too ashamed to admit it. Slowly, millimeter by millimeter, I sensed my soul being slowly peeled off the steel bones of my life. Done, it swayed like a flag, announcing to anyone willing to take the time to look, that I was a smudged rag of meaningless existence. When I finally saw the sky, mottled by trees half-finished with their knitting of branches, pour thick drops of paint on the backside of my soul, I realized why I had felt so sore all over. So many bruises had been imprinted onto me. One day I would break free of those words tainting my life and become a blank page. I would be a beautiful sheet of paper caught dancing up down sideways in the wind before falling gently into the trashcan of the cosmos. Heaven would be a dream of nothingness and love.

Raymond Luczak

Todd W Carlborn

he said hed wait for me
when i came back from
my oneonone catechism class
with a beadyeyed nun
with a turkey wattle neck
at st ignatius loyola school
on the other side of the canal
it was for only one hour
but when i came back on the van
there he was waiting on the playground
we were in third grade
seeing him smile
i didnt know that there were many kinds of love
i didnt know that i could be
allowed to feel love
so many people had manipulated me
into doing so many unwanted things
maybe because i wore hearing aids
but he never demanded anything
he stood there smiling & waiting
on some winter nights i thought of him
when i peered out from my window
overlooking the valley
with the portage lift bridge on my left
& michigan tech on my far right
& mont ripley ski hill straight ahead
at night the skiers wore headlights
to weave blurs of light down the slope
his backyard was near the foot of the ski hill
i never saw his house itself
i knew it was somewhere on royce road
because id looked up his address
in the phone book at the house
where i was staying
in houghton during the week
but which house i never knew

i imagined his house to be a sad brown affair
its black shingles with asphalt siding hung in rows
its nails slowly rusting underneath
its black tar hiding the darkness of men & women
divorce happened in that house
he was the first person i knew who had divorced parents
he never went into details just fighting all the time
just like how i never told him
about that one friday night
when i came home to ironwood from houghton
i found dad all blustered up & so angry
that he pulled out a long white rubbery tube
already flayed
he had to whup someones ass
i was too scared to watch
i heard someone yelp
we were all silenced
i never learned the details
of what happened earlier in the week
while i was gone
i was afraid to ask all weekend
my father became a ghost with sad sad sad eyes
i dont recall him asking for forgiveness
a cloud of fear hung invisibly
my eight brothers & sisters eventually started
laughing & carrying on
as if nothing happened
but i never forgot the whip
its splayed ends tucked between
the two stacks of newspapers
atop the refrigerator
i never asked todd why his parents fought
that never mattered to me
he was simply a boy who stood waiting for me
unlike my siblings who nodded hi
whenever i came home for the weekend
after five days away in houghton
he made me feel worth waiting for

Raymond Luczak

A Prayer to Uri Geller

O can you grant me the telekinesis
to bend the spines of these boys always taunting
so they'd buckle from such maleficent pain,
their bodies mere spoons?

    On late-night television,
    your hands become a vision.

O can you lend your gift of telepathy
so I won't have to strain hard to read those lips,
my brothers and sisters gibbering away
around the kitchen?

    You are accused of fraud;
    yet people still applaud.

O can you divine me like the god you are,
communicating with extraterrestrials
53,000 light years away, so I
can rise up on high?

    Your backtrackings leave me
    confused. Who'd believe me?

O can anyone else save me from all this
gobbledygook of lips moving and faces
laughing as if I'm no longer a presence
misunderstanding?

Raymond Luczak

The Doctor-Poacher
in English and ASL gloss

Look how proud you appear with your leather safari hat.
You won't tell everyone how hard it was to find it in your size.
> *hands-glide-up-down-you proud heart-inflate why s-a-f-a-r-i hat leather w-o-w
> secret won't announce hat size yours hard find wow-wow*

Watch how you can jut-jut-jut in your Jeep across the plains.
You'd never admit that holding a rifle makes you reckless.
> *hands-glide-up-down-you stiff sit j-e-e-p ride-like-horse p-l-a-i-n-s there
> secret hands-lust-throat ready shoot excite thrill*

Practice your detachment as you scan with your binoculars.
Your myopia is worse than your sight. There are no elephants.
> *hands-glide-up-down-you nothing stand binoculars sweep-landscape
> secret see-see far bad out-there elephants none*

Try to sound jaded when you turn to your Swahili guide.
You don't know this, but you've paid him not to laugh at you.
> *hands-glide-up-down-you bored stand head-nod talk guide himself s-w-a-h-i-l-i
> secret you not-know but himself hide laugh you*

Sleep under the stars and fret over missed shots.
You won't dare complain about the thinness of your blankets.
> *hands-glide-up-down-you try sleep mind-busy-busy shots miss shucks
> secret won't admit blanket thin nothing you-shiver-cold*

Strut around in your khaki shorts and look to the sun rising.
Days have become disposable like cigarette butts.
> *hands-glide-up-down-you move strut shorts k-h-a-k-i watch-watch sun rise
> every-day same-old-same-old same cigarette-smoked-to-nub throw-away*

Hunt us down to extinction if you can.
Out here in the grass, a thousand lions await.
> *hands-glide-up-down-you go-ahead search us deaf people point-ear surgery
> grass grow-tall-out-there l-i-o-n-s lions many all-over hide ready wait-wait*

Raymond Luczak

Men on the Great Plains

Their reckless hearts are tumbleweeds on fire

      rolling, flaming high, billowing with rage

bottle-stoppled as the sky turns the page

      from blue to gray to which all life expires.

Coughing in dust clouds, those men endure parch

      as they hallucinate flashes of rain.

Bit by bit their skins crumble on the plains

      and yet with their prayers, they hold steady march

for an answer, an uncorking of sky

      to relieve the sizzle of land ashen,

burned raw in the rationale of passion.

      Their wild ways are salooned with questions why

they can't answer. Yet they exchange glances

      and strike their matches. We take our chances.

Lips-Kiss-Pray Two-Together-Forever (Two People Kissing for the First Time is Always an Act of Prayer)

in ASL gloss

[*open palms only*]

long-ago
out-there
snow-fell-slowly
snow-on-ground-rose-slowly
trees out-there
snow-on-ground-rose-slowly-to-nose
skies darkened
body-shiver-cold
almost-dead
eyelids-droopy
dreams feverish

[*index fingers only*]

person-walk-distant-approach
me-thirsty
sun aim-down-at-me
rays spin-drill-between-eyes
head lightning
person-stand-tilt
person spin-fall-bounce-bounce
person-on-ground head-spinning
spin-spin-spin hallucinate

[*open palm and index finger*]

gusts wind not-matter
two-people-approaching-each-other
kiss-each-other pray
lips-kiss-pray two-together-forever

Raymond Luczak

The Burglar

Say your prayers before the last flicker of fire,

the first chill of dark moving in, a fog

of sounds unfamiliar even in your dreams,

the moon slipping in and out of mottle,

casting shadows of blue, centipedes

scurrying quicker than squirrels gathering

the last of day's fall, rabbits tossing

aside dust puffs of fright. Night's a thief.

Anything bright and shiny will be taken.

Stay still when you sleep. Night knows

of the flame sheltered in your heart.

Stay strong, and don't be afraid to dream.

An Interview with the Snow

I am sat opposite Snow.
A brown round table holds two glasses between us.
Snow has folded itself into every crease,
curve and contour of its chair.
I am in the wheelchair Snow gave me.

Two cameras point toward us,
a producer speaks into my ear.
Asks if I am ready.
I turn to the two hundred or so people
in the audience and say, *Ladies and Gentlemen*
please welcome my guest this evening
The Snow.

This will be a short interview,
two questions only.
Why do you return each year?
What do you want?

I spit the questions out; I want them to be
pellets of salt fired at Snow's surface.
Snow looks at me. That same stupid smirk
that sits on its face whenever it reappears.

Snow answers.
You still haven't learned have you?
Isn't it obvious?
I want to take you places your legs
no longer will.
I want to make you feel where dead skin now lingers.
You have started to find calmness,
you need to remember the depths
I have taken you before.

Snow is a trespasser
on my recovery.

Stephen Lightbown

Coal dot lips sit
where there used to be a smile.
I look at Snow.
When it spits cobwebs
at my window, I'm back to pulling
leg hairs. Snow's angels are left behind
rooted. I can't see out.

I look Snow straight at its cold,
empty face and say,
All of your answers may be true.
But I will still be here long after you have gone.

Under warm studio lights,
Snow has no comeback.

When We Say Goodbye, We Talk Too Fast

*A poem that talks to the poems of Zoeglossia fellows Zoe Stoller, Naomi Ortiz,
Stephanie Heit, and Margaret Ricketts*

Silence asks for two shots,
oat milk, extra hot. The usual.
The day is four hours out of bed but you wake
only when caffeine has been consumed.
You take the reusable in both hands, wrap fingers
around warming plastic like a hungry
body stretched across the shoreline.

The coffee speaks. *Tomorrow turn
away from the sun. Look
towards the moon.* I inhale
four self-measured goodbyes.

Later, when the caffeine has left,
I watch you. My ritual.

You stand in the bedroom,
that's actually an office, but really
where we keep our laundry.
You take out hair grips,
which you won't find
again. Remove dance class
glitter, moisturise.

You do all this whilst gazing out the window
at the lighthouse beam 250,000 miles
from earth. Your ritual.

Tomorrow, a passport apart, when I look
past rooftops and connect
night-sky dots,
our shadows will join.

Next week,
we'll be alive.

Stephen Lightbown

The Softening

June brings more
to us than January.

As terracotta roof tiles
occupy the view
where sand should be
a head pokes
through a skylight
like an inquisitive crab
before it disappears
for coffee
and cigarillos.

We share this view,
on hot white sheets
and fill the gaps
with senses.

An open window
provides little relief
from moped horns and
seagull caw. Heat forbids

an embrace
so we chance
a dance with
interlocking fingers.

Later the ocean turns black.
We are unmoved.
There's menace in the
margarita cheers.
Everything indistinguishable.

The sound of the swell
in the night confirms
familiar
has returned.

There's been a two year
permafrost
to our tenderness.

Here, at last,
It begins
to thaw.

Stephen Lightbown

Breathless

It started. A typed question—
Do you have wheelchair access?
Grew. A one sentence reply—
Yes, can they manage one step?
They. I did not correct.
Prised free from my paralysis,
put it to one side
with yesterday's labels.
Replaced cared for sympathy
with credit for caring.
Deceit: I had trusted myself.
Jumped,
the first chance I got.
The ground suddenly sturdy under
feet. Who is this man that stands
inside of me?
I enquire with Mozart fingers.
Feel tendons hatch from hibernation.
Feel denim against legs.
Feel thighs swell with years
of walking.
I'm out of control—
Do you ... ? Three restaurants,
a theatre, two hotels,
gin tasting. I guess I drink now too.
Out of breath from untruths.
Weightless with new footsteps.
Stop pushing.
Ask me, ask me,
What do they need?
We'll be fine,
          we are
                    quite
                              independent.
                                        Quite.

WE ARE NOT YOUR METAPHOR

Stephen Lightbown

Jump of The Needle

"The spacecraft will be encountered and the record played only if there are advanced spacefaring civilizations in interstellar space."

—Carl Sagan

A midnight go to carbonara, a half-finished
bottle of Shiraz, a last goodbye,
an aisle of smudged mascara
and paper snow-flakes.

Music jolts the memories.
Vinyl—a resting heartbeat
of 78 RPM—the reoccurring
pulse by which we move.

Pick an LP at random,
take it out of the sleeve.
Submerge your gaze into the dark sheen.
Beyond your reflection. Beyond the groove
where stylus skates across *Feeling Good*.
Dust, scratches, dead wax. Lines that circle
track listings like rings of Saturn.

Keep looking. Into the black empty.
Beyond ISS with its fifteen sunsets,
jump stepping stone asteroids
from Mars to Jupiter. Past, once a planet,
never been a planet, Pluto. Stare into interstellar
emptiness, thirteen billion miles
from what you hold in your hand.

Look with radio wave eyes.
You will see Voyager One.
A Deep Space cover that holds
the Gold Disc.

Stephen Lightbown

Released in 1977, forever on tour.
Our first extra-terrestrial
gift was a compilation album.
So typically human. The Pale Blue Dot,
make us turn.

We are
every record ever played:

fifty-five hellos, whale song,
strings of Beethoven, Chuck Berry's
onel-egged hop;

pressed. Silent. Waiting.

Electrical Work Index Series

Index Series is the term used in shock land to describe the initial 6-12 electroshocks (ECT) that generally do the trick. Then there is *continuation* and *maintenance*. My course (or their course, depending) was 30 sessions from October 2011 through March 2012.

Waiting Bay

Rows of beds with bodies wheeled down from the top floor inpatient unit to the basement. Hospital gowned, bodies to be moved, turned, tended as diagnosis codes. IV's attached to veins located and plumbed. Wristband particulars. Blood pressure cuff velcroed around right ankle. Sticky leads attached to chest. Beeping sounds from the curtained off room we wait to enter. Fear wipes out any smells. Dry mouth taste from anesthesia fast and panic.

Treatment Room

Drive-thru fast. Curtain pulled. Bed head hinged horizontal. Doctor in the corner in white. Anesthesiologist out of sight behind my head. I interrupt the oxygen mask, ask for names. Before I am ready they push sleep,

push their batons on both my temples, hit on.

Recovery Bay

Passed out bodies return from the room red, elevated blood pressures, facial twitches, mouth guards stick out lips until the nurses remove them. Check vitals. Make sure there is still breath and heart. Hold plastic containers to catch vomit. The involuntary urine and shit during a seizure will be dealt with later. Oxygen masks, paddles on standby. Before we return to the top floor, we must pass orientation tests:

Stephanie, you are waking up from ECT.
You are in the University Hospital.
Can you tell me your name?
Can you tell me where you are?

Stephanie Heit

Waiting Bay

Pincushion trial. Teaching hospital. After both residents have a go (repeat this every session) they get the nurse from another department, vein whisperer, who swoops in and taps me like a hypersensitive woodpecker finds critters in the tree trunk. She gets it, makes sure the IV flows. This time in the wrist. Fragile thin. I wait with a girl next to me from the children's unit. Just outline. Her features almost not. Wish to be invisible and ultimate desire to disappear nearly realized. We breathe the hospital basement air, antiseptic and stale, more carbon dioxide than oxygen. Not enough inhales.

Treatment Room

Going out goes hard. The meds burn in. *Shitshitshit* under my breath under the oxygen mask. They push more. Get her out. Get sleep. Get on with it. Background fear that the vein will give, anesthesia fail: I'll wake up being electrocuted. The mental health worker grabs my hand, rubs my forearm firmly—a distract sensation from the burning. Touch, usually a side effect of blood pressure cuff placement, pulse monitor, thermometer. Implements rather than skin. This is the only instance I remember someone holding my hand out of kindness. *Thank you D.*

Recovery Bay

I don't remember waking up. Don't remember the questions, the vital checks. Don't remember curling up fetal style on my side. Don't remember the elevator ride up to the 9th floor. Don't remember putting on my clothes. The see you in 3 days niceties with the ECT staff. Don't my dad pushing the wheelchair. Don't the hospital cafeteria. Don't the check out line and the pity looks. Don't the 4 hour drive home. Don't the silence.

Neuromodulation Master

I make brains quake. Bodies rupture.
Bones break. In the old days before
anesthesia and muscle relaxants.
Now it's passive city while I charge
through dead end streets, *this way
only* signs going the wrong direction.
Ordinary day of sizzle. Electrons
vibrate, a contagious undertaking.
I leave indelible marks. Not on
the temples of my charges. The
aftermath memory loss, pianists
who forget how to play, loved ones
now strangers, that sort of thing.
My charges are almost all women.
And the ones hitting the go button,
men. I'm neutral. A funny thing for
a conductor to say but my orchestra
plays the indifferent sonata. *Don't kill
the messenger* is my motto. I go where
directed. I'm held in the shaky hands
of shock virgin residents. My main
contact is with the temple and top
of head of my charges. I don't get
attached, even though some of them
return three times a week. My job is
to induce the juice, not to track my
electrical impact. I leave that to the
whitecoats. There is a movement to
ban me. Afraid of my power, no doubt.
Or the fact I'm not FDA approved. I
buzz my electroconvulsive melody,
staccato and consistent at 70-150
volts for 0.1 - 0.5 seconds. I turn that
excitable brain tissue on, light bulbs
aflicker in so much dark.

ETC. THE RESISTANCE

Written on the inside of the napkin accompanying the dinner trays for psych unit patients admitted for ECT treatment.

Located in the inpatient discharge folder thanks to a mental health worker double agent working for ETC. THE RESISTANCE. Placed behind the safety plan worksheet that is not safe.

READ THIS IN PRIVATE. SHARE WITH OTHER INMATES CAREFUL TO NOT ALERT THE KEEPERS, THE SHOCK BRIGADE

If you are receiving this note, you are in dire circumstances. Last ditch effort, any measures to keep you here. No doubt the "treatment" you are scheduled for has been touted as extremely effective with unbelievable success rates. They are unbelievable for a reason. Perhaps you watched the propaganda video with the soft colors & spa like ambience —more luxury vacation than let's shoot kilowatts through your brain & hope for the best. No doubt they reassured you the memory loss is just around the time of treatment; the side effect of long term memory loss flashed on the screen for less than a second & not spoken out loud. You are told this is your best bet. Your loved ones, at a loss for what to do, jump on board because the ones with the whitecoats & MD by their names know best.

RUN. Get up out of the gurney & get the hell out. NOW. Slip your wristband off & make like a normate out of there. You may be like I was—indifferent, deathwish ridden, an easy consent signature. Take my word. Take my body. Better, take my mind as amnesiac evidence. LEAVE. Tell them you ate food, which will buy you time. Retract your consent. If you are involuntary or a minor, we are coming to get you. At the bottom of this page is a contact. We are waiting for you. We are a tuned network nimble to alternative options, focused on thrive rather than survive, resourced & ready to receive you.

ETC. THE RESISTANCE

Acute Effects of Chronic Heroism
to Oli

I am resourceful & adaptable
as fuck, I shit you not. For

example, this morning to walk
the toy dog in my foster care

I wore black floral lace
under my activewear because

everything else was in the wash,
which I later babysat in the base-

ment with tea & magazines to avoid
running   up

& down the stairs like all you able
bodies do without a second

thought. It was amateur hour
but also trash night the first time

I ever took the little stinker around
the block, so when he popped

a squat beside a random
can, I went diving

for something, anything,
and surfaced with a sprouted

Take thou also unto thee Wheat *and* Barley
and Beans *and* Lentils *and* Millet

and Spelt *and put them in one* Ezekiel 4:9
bread sleeve on the first

Genevieve Arlie

breath. Dog food, the same going in
as coming out. By now a seasoned

veteran, today I took several
for the neighborhood, bent

down for every abandoned log
& cake we passed on our way

home and had a five-pound baggie
after half a mile. Chew on that,

bitches. And I tossed it in my own
barrel to boot. So tomorrow when

my quads are shot from all that climbing
& squatting, I'll revise this verse

in cotton undies in between
clean sheets, a puppy on my knee.

Physical Therapy

Seems I'll do anything not to
support my own weight;

seems I don't know how to
breathe. He says not to

jut my hips so as to lean
on just anything; not to corset

my lungs in the shallows
of a sucked-in gut, but to self-

stand like a mountain, to inhale
like the Buddha belly-laughs.

Here's neutral, unswayed.
It seems my ribs flare: He lays

my hand on his so I can feel
what's normal: his ribcage

      on his good side,
      on his better side,

not releasing my hand, to show me
how I should've been made. His wife,

when they met, was the right
height to lean on after a night

on the town, so he decided to
for the rest of his life. Driving

home, I detour off the highway
for the botanical garden and hike

Genevieve Arlie

down to the river where once vast
canebrakes are trying to reestablish

themselves. Through the rasp-
berry thickets I can't reach

the water, but harken to its lap
& babble, the shorebirds fluting

afternoon, the breeze fluttering
yellow. The trail wends away west

into a shimmering sun, as if the sweet-
gum trees weren't adornment enough,

but to make it back in one piece
I have to turn around here.

Castling

He claimed he hated everything
green that grew & bloomed
in spring and was sad

when hearts like mine thawed
and his still carried the torch
of frost. "The original Disney

villain": the nicest thing
his coworker ever called him
as intermittently he dims

the lamps with dusk
to encourage the mood. It's not
just me in here tonight.

The original damsel
in distress in shining
armor, I ply him, "Ash,

don't meet your end plunging
off a cliff or impaled
on a sword. Go do something

noble." "Like what?"
he replies, coldly
rose & golden in my eyes,

and smiles. Also ice
can start a fire, only he's
what's left after I go out.

Genevieve Arlie

Of late, all creatures

including most insects, excluding most
people, are almost impossibly precious

to me, the dispassion of suffering
we inflict on us almost unbearable:

carpenter ants my housemate
feeds a mixture of borax

and powdered sugar curled fetal
in one another's mouths; earwigs

striving out of torrential
rivulets in the shower, washing

out on their spineless backs.
Nightly I dream of abandon-

ed dogs and comb the local
adoption listings for one

the size of a human
newborn, one I could carry,

even if couldn't walk. A thousand miles
apart, the geometer
                & I
text each other from bed the bad
puns for which I adore him,

but he can't make up his mind,
and he can't not. I remind

myself love is not
love. What besides

the heart works its whole
life until it stops?

Ferryman's Matin

Since morning I've killed
two houseflies who trapped themselves
indoors only to languish
at the windowsill like house-
wives in the fur and lace
of mourning, licking salt from the lips
of teacups, impregnating melon
rinds in the trash; and released five lady-
bugs to an opalescent autumn, some
uniform persimmon, some
polka-dot candy apple, so at least
they didn't have to die
on their backs, wings splayed,
legs splayed, in dusty microbial
corners, but the fresh-blown
grave of the world. Whatever lures
them in from outside, they never escape
unassisted, though for now
I come & go as I please.

Genevieve Arlie

From the Tree

My father is of average stature, as men go,
and strong, as men are, and hirsute
in his ears as the years wear on, and on
his back, the skin on his hands cracked
from long hours of ungloved carpentry
and metalwork, of nosing around in the beehive
for wooden frames fat with honey,
but with certain effeminacies about him,
like his hypersensitive hearing I inherited
and his size-nine, virgin-white feet.
With peasant soles my mother plods
across the summer asphalt as he tiptoes
daintily in the mottled shade. He gave her
two daughters, and "thank god,"
she laughs. "If I'd had a son with that man,
he would've been a gay poet,
and they would've hated each other."
It's because they don't know me that I
ask: *How do I put this? Here I am.*

KATHI WOLFE is a poet and writer. Her forthcoming collection is *Love and Kumquats: New and Selected Poems* (BrickHouse Books).

VIKTORIA VALENZUELA is currently earning her MA/MFA at Our Lady of the Lake University. She is an inaugural Zoeglossia Fellow, a Macondista, and the organizer of 100 Thousand Poets for Change: San Antonio.

GAIA CELESTE THOMAS is the author of *Aloft Alight* (Antiquated Future). Her work appears on *Dispatches from the Poetry Wars* and *Godiva Speaks*. She lives in Oakland, California, and holds an MFA from Mills College.

ELIZABETH THERIOT is a poet and essayist with Ehlers-Danlos Syndrome. She advocates for reproductive justice with The Yellowhammer Fund, and is writing a memoir. [elizabeth-theriot.com]

ZOE STOLLER is a poet and copywriter. Her writing has appeared in *DIALOGIST, Glass: A Journal of Poetry, Rabbit Catastrophe Review, The New Guard, Word Riot*, and elsewhere. [zoestoller.com]

JESSICA SUZANNE STOKES has a purple wheelchair and a lot of hair. [jessicasuzannestokes.com]

MARGARET RICKETTS has studied in Provincetown, Berea College, American University, and Pine Manor College.

NAOMI ORTIZ, a disabled mestiza, is a writer, poet, visual artist, facilitator, and the author of *Sustaining Spirit: Self-Care for Social Justice* (Reclamation Press), a guide on self-care for diverse communities. [naomiortiz.com]

Contributors

RAYMOND LUCZAK is the author and editor of 22 books, including *Flannelwood* (Red Hen Press) and *Lovejets: Queer Male Poets on 200 Years of Walt Whitman* (Squares & Rebels). [raymondluczak.com]

STEPHEN LIGHTBOWN, a UK-based poet and disability rights champion, writes extensively but not exclusively about life as a wheelchair user. His debut poetry collection *Only Air* was published in 2019. [stephenlightbown.com]

STEPHANIE HEIT is a queer poet, dancer, teacher, and author of *The Color She Gave Gravity*. She is bipolar and a member of the Olimpias, an international disability performance collective. [stephanieheitpoetry.wordpress.com]

GENEVIEVE ARLIE is always a tree hugger & dog lover with chronic fatigue and currently a Ph.D. student in English—creative writing at the University of Georgia.

About Zoeglossia

Zoeglossia is a literary organization that is seeking to pioneer a new inclusive space for poets with disabilities. Much like its predecessors Canto Mundo, Kundiman, Cave Canem, and Lambda Literary, Zoeglossia strives to create a supportive community that fosters creativity. Through an annual retreat, poets from all backgrounds will have the opportunity to learn from established writers who also have disabilities, and from each other. These retreats, which poets will have the opportunity to attend three times, will promote professional development among this shared creative community.

The three-day retreat will admit a small group of writers to be mentored by prominent poets with disabilities. All attendees—teachers and students—will present their writing at a series of readings open to the public. Teachers and returning poets will provide panel discussions on professional and literary issues, roundtables, and other professional support with the emerging writers. Writers, once admitted, will be encouraged to attend three times over the following years to earn the title of "Fellow."

Zoeglossia wishes to thank the Poetry Foundation and Steve Young for the generous grant that made the first Zoeglossia Conference—and this book—possible. We also want to thank our generous donors, Arnold and Julia Bradburd of the Bradburd Family Foundation, Connie Voisine, Clay and Moira Black, Rigoberto Gonzalez and Alison Hedge Coke for their generous donations. A big thank you to our wonderful board and to the many folks at OLLU who worked so hard to make the first Zoeglossia conference a success: Dean Bill Brownsberger, Dawn Morales, Nan Cuba, Grace Sinyard, Dr. Yvette Benavidez, Dr. Leah Larson, Viktoria Valenzuela, and Dr. Octavio Quintanilla.

For more information, please go online at zoeglossia.org.

CPSIA information can be obtained
at www.ICGtesting.com
Printed in the USA
LVHW040339151019
634227LV00022B/2686/P

9 781941 960141